# Ecosystems
# Oceans

## Heather C. Hudak

www.av2books.com

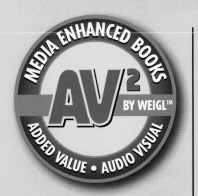

AV² provides enriched content that supplements and complements this book
Weigl's AV² books strive to create inspired learning and engage young mind
in a total learning experience.

## Your AV² Media Enhanced books come alive with...

**Audio**
Listen to sections of
the book read aloud.

**Key Words**
Study vocabulary, and
complete a matching
word activity.

Go to **www.av2books.com**,
and enter this book's
unique code.

**Video**
Watch informative
video clips.

**Quizzes**
Test your knowledge.

## BOOK CODE

### H648297

**Embedded Weblinks**
Gain additional information
for research.

**Slide Show**
View images and
captions, and prepare
a presentation.

**AV² by Weigl** brings you media
enhanced books that support
active learning.

**Try This!**
Complete activities and
hands-on experiments.

## ... and much, much more!

Published by AV² by Weigl
350 5th Avenue, 59th Floor
New York, NY 10118
Website: www.av2books.com    www.weigl.com

Library of Congress Cataloging-in-Publication Data

Hudak, Heather C., 1975-
Oceans / Heather C. Hudak.
    p. cm. -- (Ecosystems)
Includes index.
ISBN 978-1-61913-074-6 (hard cover : alk. paper) -- ISBN 978-1-61913-237-5 (soft cover : alk. paper)
1. Ocean--Juvenile literature. I. Title.
GC21.5.H83 2013
551.46--dc23
                        2011044152

Printed in the United States of America in North Mankato, Minnesota
1 2 3 4 5 6 7 8 9  16 15 14 13 12

012012
WEP060112

**Project Coordinator** Aaron Carr
**Design** Sonja Vogel

Every reasonable effort has been made to trace ownership and to obtain permission to reprint copyright material. The publishers
would be pleased to have any errors or omissions brought to their attention so that they may be corrected in subsequent printings.

Photo Credits
Weigl acknowledges Getty Images as its primary photo supplier for this title.

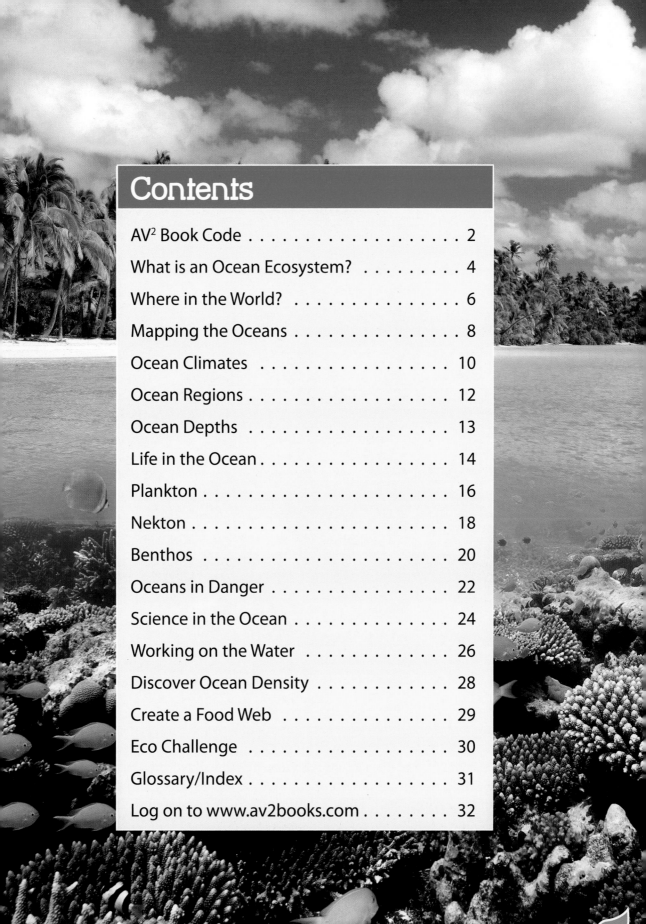

# Contents

# What is an Ocean Ecosystem?

Some fishes have striped camouflage. This makes it more difficult for predators to see the outlines of their bodies.

Earth is home to millions of different **organisms**, all of which have specific survival needs. These organisms rely on their environment, or the place where they live, for their survival. All plants and animals have relationships with their environment. They interact with the environment itself, as well as the other plants and animals within the environment. These interactions create **ecosystems**.

Oceans are a type of ecosystem. They cover 70 percent of Earth's surface, and contain 97 percent of its water. The world's five oceans are known as the Atlantic, Pacific, Indian, Arctic, and Southern Oceans. Though they are named separately, there are no physical barriers between them. They form one large body of water.

Oceans are some of the most diverse ecosystems on the planet. Many **species** have **adapted** to the wide variety of ocean conditions, from warm **tropical** lagoons, to the crushing, lightless chill of the deepest trenches.

## Levels of Organization in Ocean Ecosystems

### Organizing the Ocean

Ecosystems can be broken down into levels of organization. These levels range from a single organism to many species of organism living together in an area.

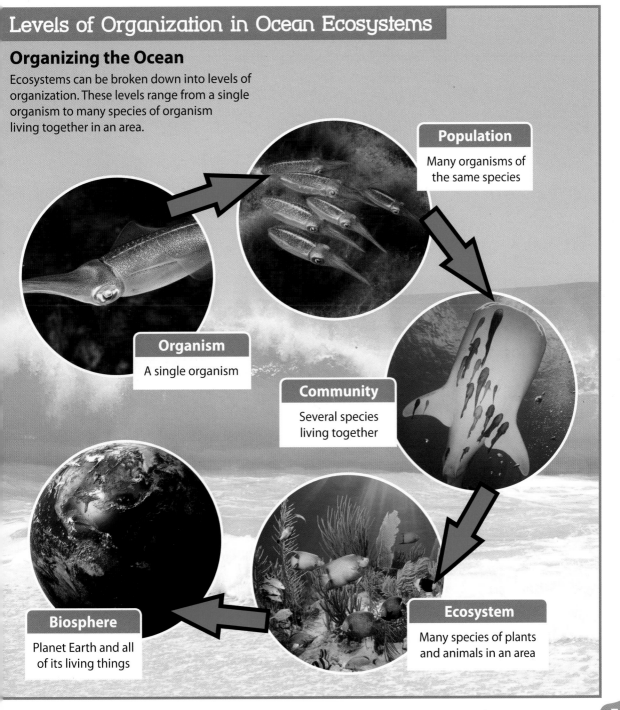

**Population**
Many organisms of the same species

**Organism**
A single organism

**Community**
Several species living together

**Ecosystem**
Many species of plants and animals in an area

**Biosphere**
Planet Earth and all of its living things

# Where in the World?

Even the ocean's sand contains many tiny organisms. Animals such as ghost crabs sift through the sand for food.

Although they are connected, each of the five oceans exists in a distinct geographic location. The Pacific Ocean, at about 64 million square miles (165 million square kilometers), is the world's largest ocean. The Pacific lies off the western coasts of North and South America. It extends to the eastern coasts of Asia and Australia.

Earth's second-largest body of water is the Atlantic Ocean. This ocean, 41 million square miles (106.5 million sq. km) in size, lies between the eastern coasts of North and South America and the western coasts of Europe and Africa.

The Indian Ocean is 28 million square miles (73.5 million sq. km) in area. Enclosed by southern Asia to the north, Africa to the west, and Australia and the Sunday Islands to the east, the Indian Ocean is the third-largest body of water in the world.

**Eco Facts**

The average depth of the ocean is 12,460 feet (3,800 meters). This is 10 times the height of New York City's Empire State Building.

The Southern Ocean circles Antarctica. It accounts for nearly 8 million square miles (20 million sq. km) of open water, making it the fourth-largest body of water on Earth. Prior to 2000, it was not referred to as an ocean itself. It was considered part of the Indian, Atlantic, and Pacific Oceans.

The smallest of the world's five oceans is the Arctic Ocean. It is 5.4 million square miles (14 million sq. km) in area. Europe, North America, Asia, and many islands border the Arctic Ocean.

In the world's polar oceans, ice forms an important, if temporary, habitat for birds and mammals.

# Mapping the Oceans

Two-thirds of Earth's surface is covered by water. This map shows where the world's oceans are located, as well as smaller areas of the oceans called seas. Find the place where you live on the map. Do you live close to an ocean? If not, which ocean is closest to you?

## Legend

 Oceans, Seas, Bays

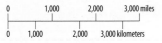 Rivers

## Scale at Equator

| 0 | 1,000 | 2,000 | 3,000 miles |
|---|-------|-------|-------------|

| 0 | 1,000 | 2,000 | 3,000 kilometers |
|---|-------|-------|------------------|

N

ARCTIC OCEAN

**Beaufort Sea**

**Bering Sea**

NORTH AMERICA

**Gulf of Mexico**

ATL. OC

EQUATOR

PACIFIC OCEAN

SOUTH AMERICA

### Pacific Ocean

**Location:** Between Asia, Australia and the Americas
**Average Depth:** 14,042 feet (4,280 m)
**Fact:** This ocean is larger than all of Earth's continents put together. It also contains the world's largest living structure, the Great Barrier Reef. This reef is 1,250 miles (2,012 km) long and can be seen from space.

### Atlantic Ocean

**Location:** Between Europe and Africa, and the Americas
**Average Depth:** 10,995 feet (3,339 m)
**Fact:** The Atlantic is the youngest of the world's oceans. It was formed around 150 million years ago, when North and South America spread apart from Africa and Europe.

SOUTHE OCEAN

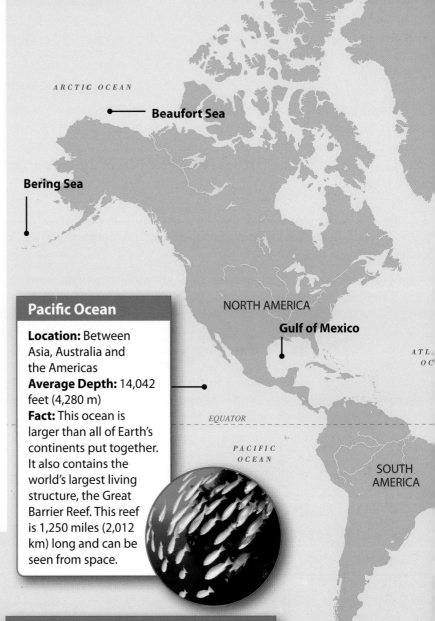

ARCTIC OCEAN

## Arctic Ocean

**Location:** Surrounding the geographic North Pole
**Average Depth:** 3,420 feet (1,042 m)
**Fact:** For hundreds of thousands of years, the Arctic Ocean has been covered year-round by ice. Now, as Earth's climate warms, scientists predict that the ocean may be ice-free during summer by the end of the century.

ASIA

**North Sea**

EUROPE

**Black Sea**

PACIFIC OCEAN

**Mediterranean Sea**

**Bay of Bengal**

**South China Sea**

**Persian Gulf**

AFRICA

**Philippine Sea**

**Arabian Sea**

INDIAN OCEAN

AUSTRALIA

**Tasman Sea**

## Southern Ocean

**Location:** Surrounding Antarctica to 60 degrees south latitude
**Average Depth:** 14,764 feet (4,500 m)
**Fact:** In the cold, oxygen-rich waters of the Southern Ocean, organisms such as squid can grow very large. The Southern Ocean is also home to unique swimming birds known as penguins.

## Indian Ocean

**Location:** Between Australia and Africa
**Average Depth:** 12,762 feet (3,890 m)
**Fact:** The Indian Ocean is the warmest of the world's oceans. These warm temperatures are hostile to plant growth. As a result, the Indian Ocean is not as rich with life as other oceans around the world.

ANTARCTICA

9

# Ocean Climates

❙ When a large amount of warm water evaporates quickly, a hurricane may form. ❙

Oceans cover much of the world, from the freezing Arctic to the warm waters of the tropics. As a result, ocean climates vary a great deal. Near polar regions, surface water temperatures dip to about 28 °Fahrenheit (−2 °Celsius), while warmer waters reach temperatures of 97°F (36°C). The average surface temperature of the all Earth's oceans is 63°F (17°C). However, in most cases, as the water becomes deeper, the temperature decreases. This occurs because the Sun is only able to heat the upper layers of the ocean, where it shines directly. The thermocline is an area where water temperature decreases greatly. The thermocline begins between 300 and 1300 feet (91 and 396 m) below the ocean's surface. In this area, temperatures drop as low as 32°F (0°C).

## Temperatures in the thermocline

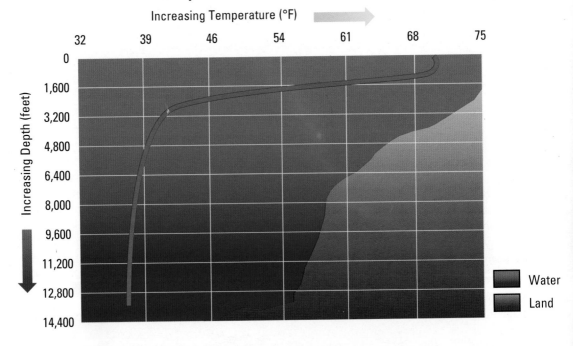

## Creating Climate Conditions

Oceans also play an important role as a driver of climate for other ecosystems. Much of the water that falls elsewhere as precipitation first **evaporated** from an ocean. The temperature of this water, and of the wind that blows it inland, has strong effects on climate worldwide.

### Eco Facts

Oceans change temperature more slowly than land. Coastal areas tend to have cool summers and warm winters as a result.

## Waves

Winds, earthquakes, volcanoes, and landslides create waves. Winds blowing across the ocean form surface waves. The size of these waves depends on how fast, how far, and for how long the wind blows. Tsunamis, or tidal waves, are huge waves that can cause great damage on land. They are caused by underwater earthquakes, volcanoes, and landslides that create shifts in the ocean floor.

## Currents

An ocean current is a continuous stream of water moving along a definite path. This stream can run vertical or horizontal to the water's surface. It can also be near the surface or deep below. Currents can be warm or cool. For example, water flowing away from the **equator** is warmer than water flowing toward the equator.

## Tides

Tides are the regular rise and fall of the level of ocean water over a certain period of time. The **gravitational pull** between Earth and the Moon causes tides. Two tides occur each day. High tide, when the water rises the furthest, is always directly beneath the Moon. Another high tide occurs on the opposite side of the globe.

As waves approach shore, they are pushed upward by the slope of the sea floor. If the shore rises smoothly and evenly, the tips of the waves may curl.

# Ocean Regions

Some whales can swim in deep waters for extended periods. However, they must return to the surface to breathe.

## Continental Shelf

Oceans surround every continent on Earth. Coastlines bordering the world's oceans slope downward at a slight angle. The angle of the slope gradually increases, leading to deeper water. This slope is called the continental shelf. In some parts of the world, the continental shelf extends many miles into the ocean. In other areas, the shelf reaches only a short distance past the shore.

## Continental Slope

The continental shelf leads to the continental slope. The continental slope is a sharp drop where the water becomes quite deep. In most areas, the continental slope begins at a depth of 430 feet (131 m). Often, the continental slope becomes a smooth, gently sloping area called the continental rise. The continental rise is part of the ocean bottom. Beyond the continental rise lies the deep ocean basin.

## Ocean Basin

The deep ocean basin is about 2.5 to 3.5 miles (4 to 5.6 km) deep on average. It covers nearly one-third of Earth's surface. The ocean's deepest reaches, known as the abyss, are located in the ocean basin. Deep-sea rifts in the ocean floor, called trenches, are also found here.

### Eco Facts

Many ocean animals live at a specific depth for their entire lives. They have adapted to the conditions of light and pressure at that depth.

# Ocean Depths

Oceans have five main zones, or depth levels, based on the level of sunlight each area receives. As depth increases, the weight of water pressing down, or pressure, increases as well. Pressures in the deep ocean can be many hundreds of times that found in surface waters.

## Epipelagic

The epipelagic, or sunlight, zone is the ocean's shallow, top layer. This layer extends about 656 feet (200 m) below the water's surface. Here, there is enough sunlight for plants to survive.

## Mesopelagic

Located 656 to 3,281 feet (200 to 1,000 m) below the ocean's surface, the mesopelagic, or twilight, zone receives very little sunlight. Plants cannot live in this region.

## Bathypelagic

Sunlight does not reach the deep ocean area known as the bathypalagic, or midnight, zone. This zone is located about 3,281 to 13,123 feet (1,000 to 4,000 m) below the water's surface.

## Abyssal

The abyssal zone, located 13,123 to 19,685 feet (4,000 to 6,000 m) below the ocean's surface, is very dark. The water in this region is near freezing temperatures.

## Hadal

The ocean's deepest trenches are called the hadal zone. This zone is located between 19,685 and 36,089 feet (6,000 and 11,000 m) below the ocean's surface. This zone is named for Hades, the Greek god of the underworld.

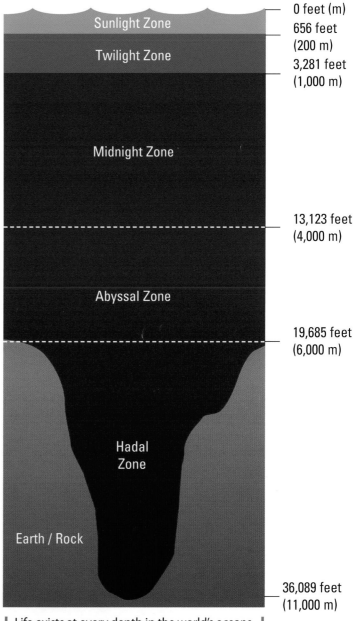

**Ocean Depth Levels**

Sunlight Zone — 0 feet (m)

Twilight Zone — 656 feet (200 m)

— 3,281 feet (1,000 m)

Midnight Zone

— 13,123 feet (4,000 m)

Abyssal Zone

— 19,685 feet (6,000 m)

Hadal Zone

Earth / Rock

— 36,089 feet (11,000 m)

Life exists at every depth in the world's oceans. Even on the deepest ocean floor, life flourishes around hot-water geysers.

# Life in the Ocean

The oceans are the cradle of all life on Earth. Life began in water, billions of years ago, and still flourishes there today. Over the history of life, oceans have supported some of the most unique creatures Earth has ever known. Today, their descendants depend on each other for the food, or energy, they need to survive. This energy transfers between organisms through the food chain.

## Producers

The plant-like organisms found in the ocean are producers for other organisms in the ecosystem. These organisms are called producers because they make their own food. They also serve as food for other organisms. Producers absorb energy from the Sun and convert it into usable forms of energy such as sugar. They make this energy through a process called **photosynthesis**. Producers found in oceans include algae, single-celled organisms called diatoms, and seaweed.

## Primary Consumers

The animals that rely on producers as a food source are called primary consumers. When a primary consumer feeds on a producer, the energy made by the producer is transferred to the consumer. Examples of primary consumers found in ocean ecosystems include small fish and **filter feeders** such as corals and clams. Even large animals such as whales can be primary consumers in an ocean ecosystem.

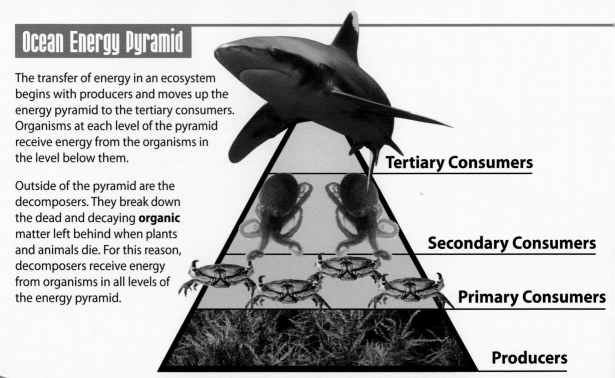

### Ocean Energy Pyramid

The transfer of energy in an ecosystem begins with producers and moves up the energy pyramid to the tertiary consumers. Organisms at each level of the pyramid receive energy from the organisms in the level below them.

Outside of the pyramid are the decomposers. They break down the dead and decaying **organic** matter left behind when plants and animals die. For this reason, decomposers receive energy from organisms in all levels of the energy pyramid.

**Tertiary Consumers**

**Secondary Consumers**

**Primary Consumers**

**Producers**

# Ocean Food Web

Another way to study the flow of energy through an ecosystem is by examining food chains and food webs. A food chain shows how a producer feeds a primary consumer, which then feeds a secondary consumer, and so on. However, most organisms feed on many different food sources. This practice causes food chains to interconnect, creating a food web.

In this example, the red line represents one food chain from the clam to the sea star and the otter. The blue line from the plankton to the barnacle, crab, and otter forms another food chain. These food chains connect at the otter, but they also connect in other places. The crab feeds on clams, and the clam may also eat plankton. This series of connections forms a complex food web.

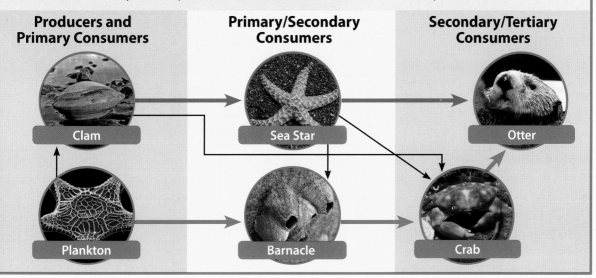

| Producers and Primary Consumers | Primary/Secondary Consumers | Secondary/Tertiary Consumers |
|---|---|---|
| Clam | Sea Star | Otter |
| Plankton | Barnacle | Crab |

## Secondary and Tertiary Consumers

Secondary consumers feed on both producers and primary consumers. In the ocean, secondary consumers include fish, reptiles and **molluscs**, such as sea turtles and snails. Crabs, squid, and some mammals, including seals, are also secondary consumers. Larger carnivores, such as sharks, and some large molluscs, including giant squid, are called tertiary consumers. Tertiary consumers feed on secondary consumers.

## Decomposers

Bottom-dwelling animals, such as crabs and urchins, and many types of bacteria live in ocean ecosystems. These organisms are called decomposers because they eat dead and decaying organic materials. Decomposers speed up the process of breaking down dead organic materials and collecting their **nutrients**. These organisms are then eaten by secondary and tertiary consumers.

# Plankton

## Free Floating

Currents, waves, and tides move tiny animals called plankton around the world's oceans. Most plankton are too small to be seen normally. Planktonic plants, or phytoplankton, absorb minerals from saltwater and energy from sunlight. They are the most common producers in ocean ecosystems. Planktonic animals, or zooplankton, serve as food for larger aquatic creatures.

## Diatoms

Diatoms are tiny organisms related to plants. They have a hard shell that sinks when they die. There are more than 10,000 diatom species. The largest individual diatoms can barely be seen without a microscope. Diatoms do not have roots, stems, or leaves. They contain chlorophyll, the substance that plants use to absorb sunlight. Diatoms often form colonies, or groups, where many organisms clump together.

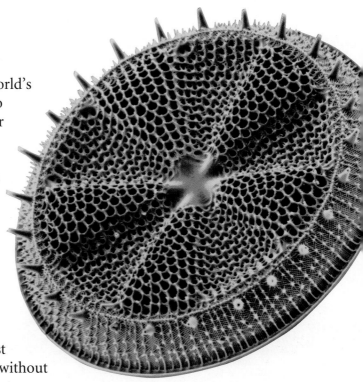

The skeletons of dead diatoms are collected and used for many purposes, such as insulation.

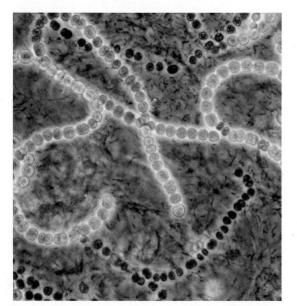

## Blue-Green Algae

Blue-green algae are bacteria that contain chlorophyll, which they use to capture sunlight and create food energy. Their proper scientific name is cyanobacteria. There are more than 800 ocean species of cyanobacteria. Most species live in fresh water. About 10 percent live in ocean environments. Like diatoms, these bacteria also form colonies. Their colonies are sometimes in the form of stringy clusters called filaments.

One of the earliest life forms on Earth was algae. Some fossils of blue-green algae are 3.5 billion years old.

# Jellyfish

Many types of jellyfish are zooplankton, moving with waves and currents. Larger ones are able to use rings of muscle in the upper part of their bodies to swim. Jellyfish are **invertebrates**. They have soft bodies which resemble jelly. Jellyfish have long tentacles that contain a poisonous venom, which they use to catch prey. There are nearly 3,000 known jellyfish species. Jellyfish do not have brains. They have a basic nervous system that senses light and chemicals in the water. Although jellyfish come in many shapes and sizes, most are bell shaped and **transparent**. They can live in many ocean environments, ranging from shallow coastal waters to depths of 12,000 feet (3,650 m).

Cells in a jellyfish's tentacles can detect touch. When prey brushes against them, these cells launch tiny, poison-tipped spines.

# Nekton

## Strong Swimmers

The best-known underwater animals are nekton. Nekton can swim against flowing currents and tides. They often live in areas where there is a specific temperature, food supply, and amount of salt in the water. Examples of nektonic animals include fish, whales, squid, and sharks.

## Sharks

More than 375 shark species live throughout Earth's oceans. They can live anywhere from the Arctic to the tropics, and in shallow or deep waters. Sharks eat almost any type of animal they find. Most sharks have triangular teeth to catch, hold, and tear prey. Other sharks, like the Port Jackson shark, have flat teeth, adapted to help them eat shelled animals such as crabs and clams. Rather than bone, shark skeletons are made from cartilage, a flexible tissue. Sharks have bodies shaped to let them swim easily. They range in length from 8 inches (20 cm) to 14 feet (4 m).

Unlike other sharks, the Port Jackson shark can breathe while eating and while floating still.

Dolphins make loud clicking noises and learn about their surroundings by listening to the echoes.

## Marine Mammals

Marine mammals are warm-blooded animals that are covered with hair or fur and breathe through lungs. Some, like dolphins and whales, have adapted to live without their fur coat. Other marine mammals include manatees, dugongs, seals, walruses, sea lions, polar bears, and sea otters. Marine mammals live in all of the world's oceans. Most marine mammals have a thick layer of fat, called blubber, between the skin and muscle. Blubber keeps these animals warm in cold waters. Manatees have only a thin layer of blubber. They live in waters no cooler than 70°F (21°C), in and around the tropics. Most marine mammals eat fish, squid, shellfish, or even other marine mammals. Sirenians, a group that includes manatees and dugongs, are the only herbivorous, or plant-eating, marine mammals.

## Eco Facts

Many large sharks are apex predators, meaning they have no natural predators. Apex predators are very imortant in healthy ecosystems. They keep the populations of primary and secondary consumers from growing too large. When there are too many primary consumers, there is a risk they will exhaust the supply of producers. The lack of food causes the primary consumers to die off. Eventually, the ecosystem that depends on them may collapse.

## Sea Turtles

There are seven sea turtle species. A sea turtle is a large, cold-blooded animal with four flipper-like limbs that it uses to swim through water and walk on land. A turtle's body is also surrounded by a shell. The top of this shell, called the carapace, varies in color, length, and shape. Sea turtles range in size from 2 to 7 feet (1 to 2 m) long. They live in tropical and temperate waters. In their early years, sea turtles live near shore. They spend the remainder of their lives in the open ocean. During the breeding season, they may travel to their nesting grounds, which are located at the same place the turtle hatched. Most sea turtles are carnivores, eating crabs, shrimps, lobsters, small fish, and jellyfish. Sea turtles do not have teeth, but their jaws are adapted to eat certain foods. The hawksbill has a beak, which it uses to find food in crevices and coral reefs. Adult green turtles are the only herbivorous sea turtles. Their jaws have serrated edges to tear apart plant materials. Other sea turtles have powerful jaws that crush prey.

Sea turtles are often victims of water pollution. They can easily mistake discarded plastic bags for the jellyfish they normally eat. Eating plastic can cause sea turtles to choke and drown.

# Benthos

## Bottom Dwellers

Animals and plants that live on the ocean floor make up the benthos. Some benthic animals, such as oysters, remain in one place their entire lives. Others, such as sea stars and lobsters, move by swimming or walking. Benthic plants can only grow in the epipelagic zone near land.

## Sea Anemones

Sea anemones are invertebrates that come in many shapes, sizes, and colors. There are more than 1,000 species of sea anemones. Most are small—reaching only 1 to 4 inches (2.5 to 10 cm) across. Others can grow up to 5 feet (1.5 m) across. Each sea anemone has a vase-shaped body. Stinging tentacles surrounding the mouth protect sea anemones from predators and capture prey. Since they cannot move, anemones wait for prey to approach before stinging it with their poisonous tentacles. The anemone's tentacles then move the prey toward its mouth. Sea anemones can live in any part of the ocean. They are most common in tropical waters, where they attach to the ocean floor, reefs, and corals, or burrow beneath the sand and mud.

Anemones are most closely related to jellyfish. Their tentacles contain the same poison-tipped stingers.

Sunflower stars are aggressive predators. They feed on urchins and other sea stars.

## Sea Stars

More than 1,800 species of sea stars live in Earth's oceans. The largest variety of species live in the Pacific Ocean. Most of these invertebrate animals have five hollow arms covered with spines on top and rows of tiny, tube-like feet on the bottom. These "feet" have suction cups, which the sea stars use to slowly move and grab onto objects. Most sea stars are about 8 to 12 inches (20 to 30 cm) across. They can range in size, however, from 0.4 inches (1 cm) to 26 inches (66 cm). Sea stars eat a variety of animals, including mussels and clams.

# Crustaceans

Crustaceans are invertebrates. There are more than 30,500 known crustacean species on Earth. They are the most populous group of species in the ocean. Many crustaceans are small planktonic organisms, such as copepods or brine shrimp. Some, like crabs and lobsters, are much larger. These animals are benthic. Crustacean bodies are divided into three parts. These are the head, the **thorax**, and the **abdomen**. Their bodies have no bones. Instead, they have a hard **exoskeleton**. They also have a segmented body. This means that parts of their body, such as the joints in their legs, are made up of similar, repeating parts. Crustaceans have two pairs of antennae that they use to smell, and legs, for swimming or walking. They also have a pair of eyes and a pair of mandibles, or jaws.

## Eco Facts

Away from coastlines, benthic animals tend to gather where nutrients are plentiful. When a dead whale sinks to the ocean floor, crabs, urchins, and other scavengers such as eel-like hagfish will live in and around the carcass for months at a time. When the whale has been completely consumed, the animals move on.

Many species of crab are intertidal. This means that they live in areas covered by water at high tide, and are exposed to the air at low tide.

# Oceans in Danger

**A**nimals in danger of becoming extinct are classified as endangered. This means there are so few of the species alive that they need protection to survive. The blue whale, hawksbill turtle, bluefin tuna, and shortnose sturgeon are just a few of the animals considered to be endangered. In the United States, people are not allowed to hunt or harm endangered animals.

Human destruction of habitats and pollution threaten the world's oceans. Pollution increases nitrogen gas levels in the water, causing large amounts of algae to grow. In coral reefs, this is particularly dangerous. Excessive algae prevents necessary sunlight from reaching the reefs, killing ocean habitat and the fish dependent on it for survival.

In other cases, overharvesting endangers certain underwater animals. Overharvesting means that too many animals are hunted. When this happens, there are not enough animals left to maintain the population. Shark fins, meat, and livers are in great demand for food or health and beauty ingredients, putting many shark species at risk of becoming endangered. Bluefin tuna meat is considered a delicacy in many places around the world, and its populations are declining rapidly. Southern sea otters were once overhunted for their furs. Today, these animals are protected from such overharvesting.

## Timeline of Human Activity in Oceans

People living in what is now Kuwait traveled the waters in boats made of woven reeds.

The Greek philosopher Aristotle is the first to record the use of a **diving bell**.

Viking explorers cross the North Atlantic from what is now Sweden and Norway. They establish colonies in Iceland, Greenland, and North America.

| 4000 BC | 1000 BC | 360 BC | 208 AD | 900 | 1519 |
|---------|---------|--------|--------|-----|------|

**Polynesian** people using canoes and wooden planks ride the waves for transportation and recreation. This is thought to be the origin of surfing.

Cao Cao, leader of China's Wei kingdom, leads his fleet in the Battle of Red Cliffs, one of the most famous naval battles in the ancient world.

Ferdinand Magellan departs on the first expedition to sail around the world. Magellan does not survive the trip, but his fleet is successful.

Bluefin tuna are heavily overfished. This apex predator faces extinction if no changes are made to fishing practices.

Marquis de Jouffroy sails the world's first working steamship. It is destroyed by its powerful engines within 15 minutes.

The RMS *Titanic*, the largest cruise ship in the world at the time, hits an iceberg and sinks on her first voyage.

Jacques Piccard and U.S. Navy Lieutenant Don Walsh descend to the deepest point on Earth, at a depth of 35,814 feet (10,916 m).

**1783**   **1845**   **1912**   **1944**   **1943**   **1960**

British explorer Sir John Franklin attempts to find the **Northwest Passage.** He and his crew are trapped by harsh weather, and die.

The largest naval battle of World War II takes place between American and Japanese naval forces near Leyte Island in the Philippines.

Jacques Cousteau and Emile Gagnan develop a **SCUBA** system, allowing divers to stay underwater longer and more safely.

# Science in the Ocean

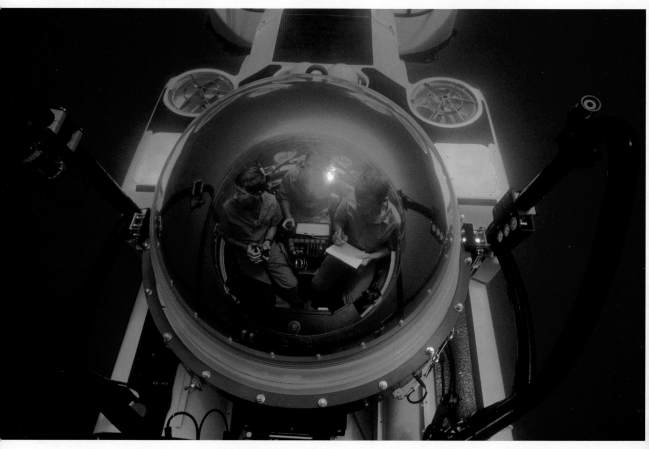

Manned research submersibles use a great deal of power. New battery technology is improving the amount of time researchers can stay underwater.

For centuries, the mysteries of the oceans have drawn the curious and the adventurous alike. Explorers and early scientists studied the environment beneath the water's surface. Today's scientists continue to study oceans. They look for ways to use the oceans' resources while preserving healthy ecosystems. Scientists continually develop new technologies for ocean exploration and research.

## Seeing With Sound

In 1822, using a basic underwater bell, Daniel Colloden discovered he could accurately measure the speed of sound underwater. Since then, technology that makes use of sound waves has advanced greatly. Scientists now know that sounds behave differently in unique ocean environments. They use devices called sonar systems to create sound waves. These waves bounce off objects in the water. Scientists can then calculate the distance between two objects in the water by measuring the time it takes for a sound to bounce between the objects. Sonar helps scientists measure the size, location, and motion of underwater objects. With enough sonar data, scientists can map the ocean and its features.

## Abyssal Evidence

Scientists use a variety of special equipment to acquire information about the ocean. Since the ocean floor has never been touched, it is one of the best indicators of Earth's history. Scientists obtain samples of the sand and mud on the ocean floor by using special drills. This is called core drilling. Scientists study core samples to learn about ocean physics, biology, and chemistry. Core drilling has helped scientists gain valuable information about sea levels and the movement of Earth's crust.

### Eco Facts

Radio tagging is one method scientists use to learn about animals. Researchers catch animals and attach electronic tags to them, before releasing them into the wild. The tags then broadcast radio signals, which help scientists track the animals' movements.

## Submersible Science

Scientists often use underwater vehicles called submersibles to enter cold, dark ocean areas. These areas are under large amounts of pressure because they are so deep in the ocean. Using submersibles, scientists examine great depths. They can uncover new ecosystems and species. Scientists also use vehicles operated by remote control to collect data. The vehicles collect samples and take photographs in areas people cannot access. These vehicles then send television signals to scientists aboard ships.

Research submersibles use small engines called thrusters to help them move in any direction.

# Working on the Water

Ecologists use quadrats to measure how many organisms live in a certain area of the sea floor.

From working with whales to guiding submersible vehicles through the abyss, or from developing research devices to collecting core samples, marine careers are exciting and challenging. Marine careers require a background in math, science, and computer operation. Before considering a marine career, it is important to research career options and visit marine centers that offer hands-on experiences.

## Marine Biologist

### Duties

Study ocean life and how ocean organisms interact with their environments

### Education

Bachelor of science, masters or doctorate in marine science

### Interests

Oceanography, biology, ecology, the environment

Marine biologists enjoy learning about organisms and their environments. To understand how animals and plants interact with their environments, marine biologists must also study chemical, physical, and geological oceanography. The ocean is filled with many different creatures, so most marine biologists choose to study a specific subject.

## Other Ocean Jobs

### Oceanographer

Study the physical properties of the ocean, including its geology, and the water itself

### Marine Engineer

Develop devices and technologies to assist in the oceangoing work of other professions

### Fisheries Officer

Ensure the protection of sensitive ocean ecosystems by monitoring fishing practices

### Marine Photographer

Use specialized underwater equipment to document the natural beauty of the ocean and display it for people around the world

## Jacques-Yves Cousteau

Jacques-Yves Cousteau (1910–1997) is possibly the world's most famous oceanographer. Starring in more than 115 films about the ocean and its inhabitants, and producing more than 50 books, Cousteau inspired curiosity and wonder in millions of people.

His contributions to ocean exploration did not stop at education, however. Cousteau was also an inventor. He was responsible for one of the most important innovations in aquatic research. In 1943, he and engineer Emile Gagnan developed the aqualung. This system, based on Cousteau's original design, is now the most commonly-used air supply for divers around the globe. In addition, Cousteau worked with engineers to develop a new type of sail called a Turbosail. Turbosails use large fans to make air flow more smoothly around the sail. This increases the amount of push provided by the wind.

Cousteau's work promoting science and protecting the environment did not go unnoticed. He was made a member of the U.S. Academy of Sciences, awarded the Presidential Medal of Freedom, and given the International Environmental Prize by the United Nations. Even today, people join the Cousteau Society and Team Cousteau to honor his memory, and to support his goal of keeping the world's oceans healthy and vibrant.

# Discover Ocean Density

**D**ensity is a measure of how much mass is contained in a certain space. Sea water is much more dense than the same amount of fresh water, because of the salt dissolved in it. Try this experiment to see how density might effect sea life.

## Materials

two glass jars        water        salt

measuring cup        two eggs

1    Fill both jars with the same amount of water.

2    Add a ¼-cup of salt to one jar. Stir until the salt is completely dissolved.

3    Gently place an egg in each jar.

4    Compare how the eggs float in the fresh water and the salt water. Which floats higher in the water?

## Results

The salt and other minerals dissolved in sea water increase its density. The more dense the fluid, the easier it is for other substances to float in it. This is why one egg floated higher in the water than the other. Organisms living in salt water require different adaptations for swimming than those living in fresh water because of this difference in **buoyancy**.

# Create a Food Web

Use this book, and research on the Internet, to create a food web of ocean ecosystem producers and consumers. Start by finding at least three organisms of each type—producers, primary consumers, secondary consumers, and tertiary consumers. Then, begin linking these organisms together into food chains. Draw the arrows of each food chain in a different color. Use a **red** pen or crayon for one food chain and **green** and **blue** for the others. You should find that many of these food chains connect, creating a food web. Add the rest of the arrows to complete the food web using a pencil or **black** pen.

Once your food web is complete, use it to answer the following questions.

**1** How would removing one organism from your food web affect the other organisms in the web?

**2** What would happen to the rest of the food web if the producers were taken away?

**3** How would decomposers fit into the food web?

## Sample Food Web

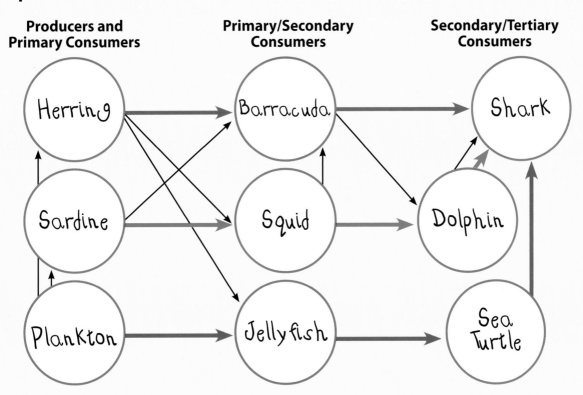

| Producers and Primary Consumers | Primary/Secondary Consumers | Secondary/Tertiary Consumers |
|---|---|---|
| Herring | Barracuda | Shark |
| Sardine | Squid | Dolphin |
| Plankton | Jellyfish | Sea Turtle |

# Eco Challenge

1. How many oceans does Earth have? Name them.

2. What is the world ocean's average surface temperature?

3. What are the three major types of the motion of water?

4. Which of the ocean's zones is the deepest?

5. To which three groups, based on movement through the water, do ocean animals belong?

6. What is the specific name for animals that have no natural predators?

7. What is the name for the material that makes up a shark's skeleton?

8. How many sea turtle species live on Earth today?

9. What three body parts do all crustaceans have?

10. Name at least two ways that ocean species become endangered.

## Answers

1. Five; Arctic, Atlantic, Indian, Pacific, Southern
2. 63°F (17°C)
3. Waves, currents, and tides
4. The hadal zone
5. Plankton, nekton, and benthos
6. Apex predators
7. Cartilage
8. Seven
9. Head, thorax, and abdomen
10. Overharvesting, pollution, habitat destruction

# Glossary

**bdomen:** the part of the body where the
igestive organs are located

**dapted:** changed over time to suit conditions

**uoyancy:** a measure of how well a given
bject floats

**iving bell:** a closed-topped metal cylinder
hat traps air, allowing a person to walk on
he sea floor

**cosystems:** communities of living things
haring an environment

**quator:** an imaginary line drawn around
arth's center

**vaporated:** turned from liquid to a vapor

**xoskeleton:** a hard outer casing which
ipports muscles and organs

**lter feeders:** animals that strain small
articles of food from the water

**ravitational pull:** a pulling force between
ny two objects, in proportion to their size

**invertebrates:** animals that do not
have backbones

**molluscs:** a group of soft-bodied animals,
including snails, squid, and clams

**Northwest Passage:** a route through the Arctic
from Europe to Asia

**nutrients:** substances that feed plants
or animals

**organic:** made up of living things

**organisms:** living things

**photosynthesis:** the process in which a green
plant uses sunlight to change water and carbon
dioxide into food for itself

**Polynesian:** relating to the peoples or cultures
inhabiting Pacific islands

**SCUBA:** Self-Contained Underwater Breathing
Aparatus, a portable air supply for divers

**species:** a group of similar animals that can
mate together

**thorax:** the segment of a crustacean's body to
which the limbs attach

**transparent:** allowing light to pass through

**tropical:** relating to the warm areas near the
equator known as the tropics

# Index

# Log on to www.av2books.com

AV[2] by Weigl brings you media enhanced books that support active learning. Go to www.av2books.com, and enter the special code found on page 2 of this book. You will gain access to enriched and enhanced content that supplements and complements this book. Content includes video, audio, weblinks, quizzes, a slide show, and activities.

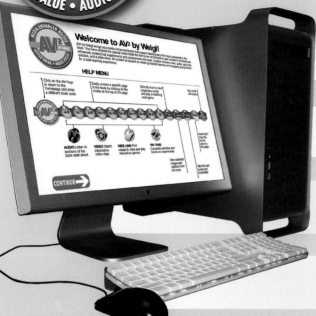

### Audio
Listen to sections of the book read aloud.

### Video
Watch informative video clips.

### Embedded Weblinks
Gain additional information for research.

### Try This!
Complete activities and hands-on experiments.

# WHAT'S ONLINE?

|  Try This! |  Embedded Weblinks |  Video | EXTRA FEATURES |
|---|---|---|---|
| Complete an activity to test your knowledge of the levels of organization in a ocean ecosystem. | Find out more information on ocean ecosystems. | Watch a video about ocean ecosystems. |  **Audio** Listen to sections of the book read aloud. |
| Complete an activity to test your knowledge of energy pyramids. | Learn more about the animals that live in ocean ecosystems. | Watch a video about animals that live in ocean ecosystems. |  **Key Words** Study vocabulary, and complete a matching word activity. |
| Create a timeline of important events in ocean ecosystems. | Find out more about the plants that grow in ocean ecosystems. | |  **Slide Show** View images and captio and prepare a presentat |
| Write a biography about a scientist. | Read about current research in ocean ecosystems. | |  **Quizzes** Test your knowledge. |
| | Learn more about threats facing ocean ecosystems. | | |

**AV[2] was built to bridge the gap between print and digital. We encourage you to tell us what you like and what you want to see in the future.**

**Sign up to be an AV[2] Ambassador at www.av2books.com/ambassador.**